# ✂ Hip Snips ✂

# Hip Snips

## Your Complete Guide to Dazzling Pubic Hair

BY PABLO MITCHELL

**QUIRK BOOKS**

PHILADELPHIA

Library of Congress Cataloging in Publication Number: 2009937554

ISBN: 978-1-59474-456-3

Printed in China
Typeset in Cooper Black and Gill Sans

Designed by Doogie Horner
Illustrations by Headcase Design
Production management by John J. McGurk

Cover photography by Jimi Robinson

Distributed in North America by Chronicle Books
680 Second Street
San Francisco, CA 94107

10 9 8 7 6 5 4 3 2 1

Quirk Books
215 Church Street
Philadelphia, PA 19106
www.irreference.com
www.quirkbooks.com

# Table of Contents

# Introduction

The fashion industry is constantly evolving and changing, looking itself in the mirror and saying, "This needs to be smaller! This needs to be bigger! This needs to go up my nose!" And I feel the world is now ready for one of the biggest changes of all: pubic art.

We style our hair, faces, shirts, pants, undies, shoes, and even socks. So why wouldn't we style our personal crotch canvases? Because narrow minds have a knee-jerk reaction to our "hair downstairs"; they see it as something gross and unmentionable. In fact, the mere mention of the word *pubic* is enough to elicit disgust. This, I feel, is a travesty. Pubic hair is a natural part of the human body and should be treated with the same reverence that we treat the rest of our bodies. Hair is hair, and hair is fabulous! And don't you owe it to your pleasure organs to decorate and celebrate them properly? After all, look at what they've done for you!

I have devoted my entire career to the styling of pubic hair, and this book is meant to enlighten the world about the beauty and styling possibilities contained deep in each and every one of our crotch patches. Read it and you will appreciate every new fun zone you encounter as beautiful in its own unique way—much like a snowflake.

While I've included my top 50 favorite pubic hairstyles for you to experiment with, I encourage you to see this not as a complete list of possible styles, but rather as inspiration for your own self-expression.

Now dive right in and make your patch pube-tastic!

# A History of Pubic-Hair Maintenance

**M**any people believe that pubic hair is a modern nuisance, a follicular inconvenience that cropped up sometime during the eighteenth century. Well, the little-known truth is that pubic hair has been around since the dawn of man—some primordial species even had pubic hair. And although today we maintain our downstairs to make a fashion statement, many early civilizations altered their pubic regions for a variety of no-nonsense reasons, including medical, religious, cultural, professional, and a preference for an acomoclitic ("smoothie") lifestyle.

In ancient Egypt, depilation (the act of removing pubic hair) was commonly utilized to combat lice infestation. Pyramids, shmiramids—the Egyptians knew that pubic-hair maintenance was the key to a burgeoning empire. With primitive tweezers, they would pluck out individual hairs, one by one, until achieving an acomoclitic state. The ancient Greeks and Romans also commonly removed all of their body hair.

And it's not just sexy loin-clothed cultures that used their personal patch as a canvas. A particularly clothed culture, Muslims believe that all adults should remove their pubic hair (and underarm hair) as a hygienic measure. The practice of pubic-hair maintenance traveled with Islam to northern Africa and surely made its way to Europe. And once you go Euro, you've got a full-blown trend!

Kings, queens, artists, priests—pubic hair was the talk of the continent. Throw in a dash of Victorian-era prudishness, and pubic-hair art had all the makings of a full-blown revolution.

By the twentieth century, lovers worldwide were expressing themselves on their personal canvases. In the 1930s, Baron Martin Stillman von Brabus shaved the pubic hair of his lover Margaret, Duchess of Argyll, into a representation of the Mercedes-Benz logo.

Yes, pubes and pop culture will forever be linked, and today, with my help, Landing Strips, Bea Arthurs, and Chewbaccas will be comingling out in the open. Viva la Pubic Revolución!

# Hair Care

Before an artist creates a masterpiece, he or she must prepare the canvas. Doing so might entail stretching the canvas to the right size or priming the canvas with gesso. And in order to style the most fabulous creation on your very own personal canvas, you must maintain and care for your hair.

In a world of disposable razors, at-home waxing kits, moisturizing conditioners, and hand-held showerheads, there's no excuse for an unattended crotch canvas. If you want to style patches that are pleasing to the eye and to your lover, some of you may need to undergo some routine maintenance. You'll need to keep your love canvas and surrounding areas generally tidy. Sure, some advanced styles require growing out your region, but you need to delineate a region in the first place if you're going to showcase superior pubic art.

## SHAMPOO VERSUS SOAP

It's a personal choice everyone must make: Do I use soap or shampoo? Surely soap will clean your canvas. And yes, shampoo will leave your patch clean and freshly scented. However, if you have sensitive skin, sometimes shampoo can be too stringent on your follicular situation. I always advise first-time artists to begin with a mild soap and move up to the more heavily scented shampoo alternatives.

## TO CONDITION OR NOT TO CONDITION

A dollop of moisturizing conditioner might be the difference between a tangle-free lustrous mane and a bland, flat set of pubes. I almost always vote "Yes" for conditioner usage, but don't fool yourself—if your patch is particularly coarse, all the conditioner in the world isn't going to help. In this case, you could try shaving it all off and seeing if something better and more manageable grows back in.

# Pubic Hairstyles

# The Short Trim

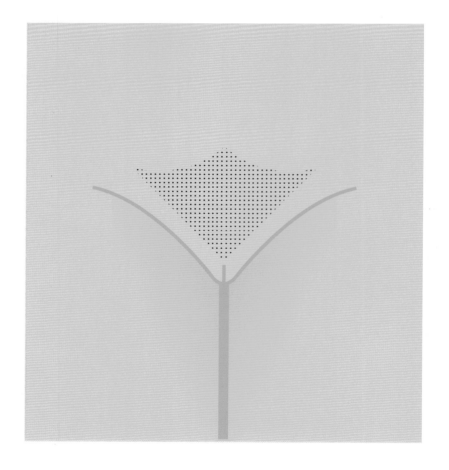

**L**ike a refreshing Coke or a slice of pizza, there's something classic and dependable about the Short Trim. And like a fine mahogany table, the Short Trim is practical, classy, and nice to lean against. A man or woman sporting the Short Trim says to the world, "I'm clean, I'm safe, and I don't have to take prescription meds to control a psychiatric condition." It allows easy access without looking too "done."

For a proper Short Trim, use an electric razor with a #1 (⅛-inch) blade guard to achieve a consistent length. You must shear the entirety of your crop into a tight, neat, even length. Trim your patch in four vertical strips, always shaving in the direction of the hair growth. Maintain with biweekly trimmings.

# The Long Trim

**W**here the Short Trim says you're all business, the Long Trim lets your freak flag fly. This is the style for the carefree flower child. Whether your natural locks are straight, curly, or downright kinked, the Long Trim says, "Dive in! And don't be afraid to stick around for a while."

To achieve the Long Trim, just let your mane grow and do a straight, simple cut.

Select a length that corresponds to your level of carefree-ness—at least two inches puts you in Long Trim territory; anything less and you're in a nebulous middle ground between short and long. Don't waver—pick a length and go with it!

# The Brazilian

**B**razil is the land of long, glorious beaches and plastic surgery on every street corner. And while the word *Brazilian* used to be an adjective, it's now a glorious noun that means "smooth as a nine-year-old."

To obtain the Brazilian, you can visit your local salon, drop your pants, and bite down on that bullet in your mouth. Or buy a quality at-home waxing kit and follow these steps:

Cover the entire area with wax. I'm talking the whole enchilada—bikini line, labia, anus . . . anywhere you see hair. Yank, yank, yank off those wax strips. Scream if you have to (and you will). Stare at the glory of your sweet, sweet naked self. Touch it. Go ahead. Not enough o's in smooooooth, huh?

# The Landing Strip

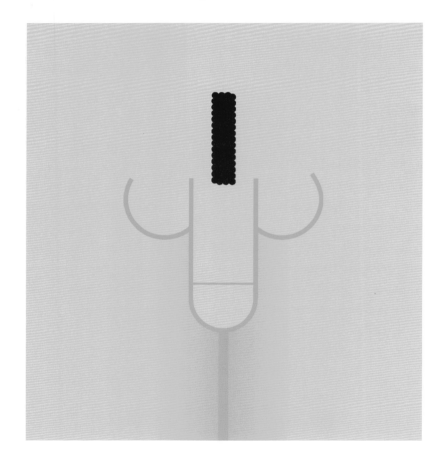

**E**asy like Sunday morning, the Landing Strip is classic, simple, and refined. This oldie-but-goodie has directed generations of men to the prize in his lady's panties, but I see no reason why a male can't sport the Landing Strip, if he's so inclined.

To style the Landing Strip, remove all your pubic hair except for a central vertical strip that extends from the top of your natural hairline to the top of your naughty bits. Keep it wide or go skinny, but never let the tarmac exceed one and a half inches or fall below a quarter inch.

With a properly finessed Landing Strip, you're sure to become a card-carrying member of the mile-high club.

# The Dong Lengthener

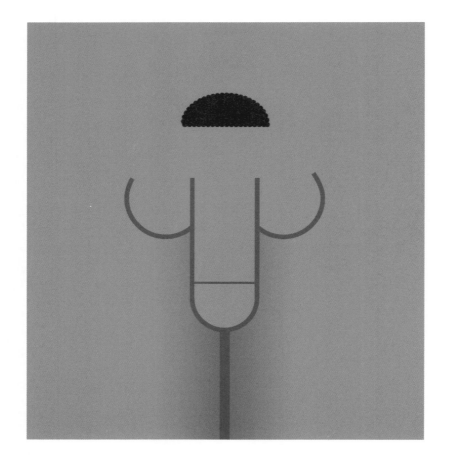

**I**f you're a man with an e-mail address, you surely get bombarded with spam advertising ways to increase your wang size. As someone highly susceptible to the marketing tactics of the penis-enhancement industry, I've tried every pill, pump, cream, and back-alley Mexican surgery that exists, so I say this from experience: There's no easier or safer way to make your dong look bigger than the optical illusion brought about by proper pubic-hair maintenance.

First, make sure your bush is cropped closely enough to expose your entire unit; you don't want any part of your dong hidden. Next, shave your region so that hair covers only a relatively small surface area. Why? Because, when judging the size of your member, your lover will compare it to the size of your bush, and if you have a tiny bush, your unit will look huge. Finally, glue a tiny racecar to your stomach, so you'll always be remembered as the dude whose dong is bigger than a car. And that's a good way to be remembered.

# The Au Naturel

**I** f you came of age in the '70s, or just wish you did, the Au Naturel is the style for you. To create it, just let yourself be as your creator made you. Don't shave, trim, or even contemplate. Just leave it alone—preferably for years. And don't be afraid to really pouf this style out. Go to the beach and let your swimsuit display the bumps, lumps, and "sideburns" of your lifestyle.

Now, you might be asking, isn't this style the same as the Long Trim? The answer is in the style's name—there's no *trimming* involved here. Use the time you used to spend on pubic-hair maintenance to start a food co-op in your community!

# The Chia Pet

**T**he Chia Pet is inspired by those cute, sprouting terracotta figurines. Like Mr. T and Gary Coleman, Chia Pets are a relic of another time, and they're ready for a comeback . . . on your crotch.

To style the Chia Pet, shave, wax, or Nair your entire pubic region to create a blank canvas. Then, take a stencil of your favorite shape—be it Homer Simpson, Daffy Duck, or, what the hell, Mr. T *and* Gary Coleman—and, with a fine marker, outline the stencil shape onto the upper portion of your crotch. Once you've drawn the desired shape, just sit back and let nature take its course. Of course, you'll have to shave and maintain the areas outside the stencil. But the fun of the Chia is watching it grow! Ch-ch-ch-chia!

# The Rat Tail

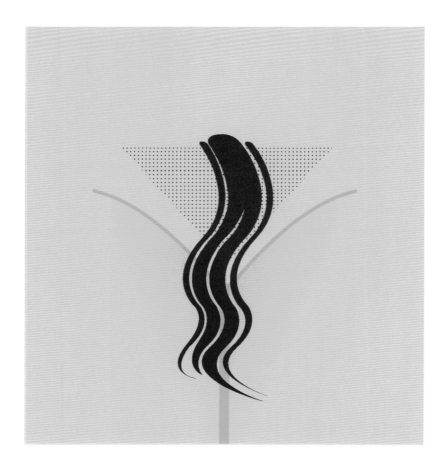

**I**f you're a redneck, a manga fan, or simply miss the '80s, the Rat Tail just might grab your downstairs fuzz fancy. It's the closest your area will get to the "business in the front, party in the back" vibe of the mullet.

For this style, shave almost all your pubic hair, leaving a small patch. Now, the placement of this patch is up to you—toward the bottom, the top, or the middle of your bush—but I highly suggest that your patch run along the centerline of your body. Otherwise it'll be visually disorienting to any visitors down there. Use styling gel to straighten and lengthen the hair of your rat tail. Then, feel free to dye or braid it. After that just sit back and wait for your lover to grab hold!

# The Hitler

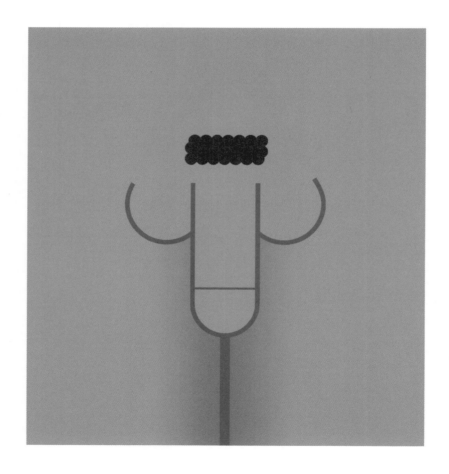

**M**any people have a negative reaction when they see the name of this late Nazi leader. And I think those negative reactions are justified. After all, was Adolf Hitler a good guy? No. But did he have a pretty sweet 'stache? Abso-freakin'-lutely.

To obtain the Hitler, shave most of your pubic hair, leaving a tightly trimmed square centered directly above your private parts. The square should be about one inch by one inch, but feel free to play with the dimensions and see what size best matches your crotch. Then just sit back and wait for your lover to invade Poland.

# The Fiddler on the Roof

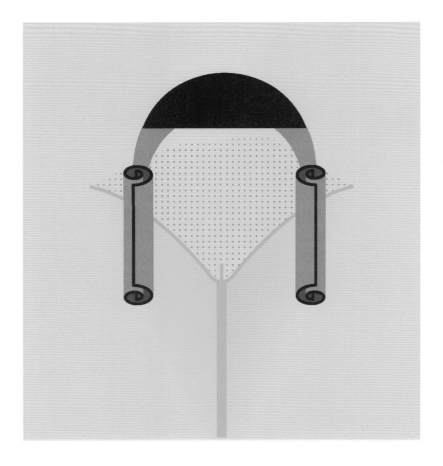

**D**oes your lover only eat kosher? Then consider the pubic peyes (long ribbons of hair that stream down from the sideburns of very devout Jews) required for the Fiddler on the Roof.

To style the Fiddler on the Roof, shave down the majority of your pubic hair, leaving full-length hair only on the left-most and right-most edges of your crotch. Grow this hair as long as it can go, and use a little styling gel to fashion each side into long ribbons. If you really want to get meshugenuh, glue a miniature yarmulke to the area between your peyes, and your lover will be on that from sunrise to sunset. *L'chaim*!

# The Bea Arthur

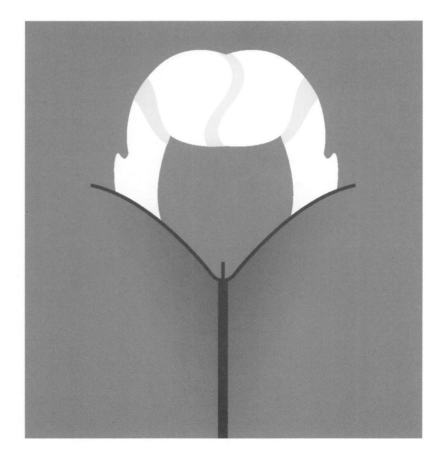

**T**hough it saddens me to say that Bea Arthur has moved on to the next episode, I'm happy to teach you how to give her props by creating your own downstairs homage to that tall, ballsy drink of water known for her glorious silver lady-bob.

First, grow out your mane two to three inches. Keep it round and contained in the middle of your crotch. Next, you'll need to match Bea's silver and white tones. If you're naturally blessed with a salt 'n' pepper patch, you're golden, girl (get it?). If not, experiment with silver, white, and gray hair coloring. Once the length and color requirements have been met, make sure you showcase that patch with attitude—walk around like you're six feet tall with a wisecrack at the ready. That's how Bea rolled.

# The Flavor Flav

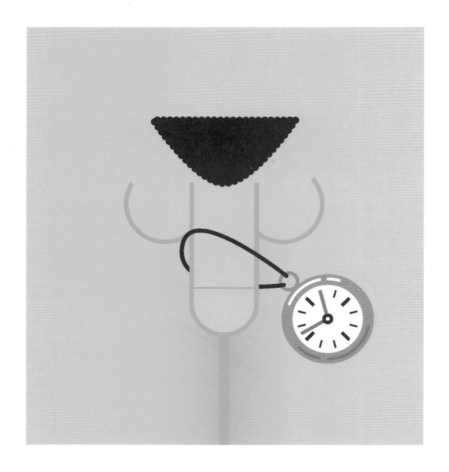

**I**s your crotch ready for the kind of comeback Flav's career has had lately? Yeah, boyee!

The Flavor Flav is really more about accessorizing than hairstyling, and Flav's best-known accessory is his hanging clock necklace. But you probably want to wear pants at some point in your life. So use a pocket watch instead, and try bedazzling it with some bling. Personally, I've been known to sport a pink rhinestone mini-clock. If you want to crank it up, you can experiment with a variety of faux-gold pubic grills. Sure, all this jewelry can be cumbersome, but if you get any complaints from your lover, well, mother-fuck him *and* John Wayne.

# The Trustafarian

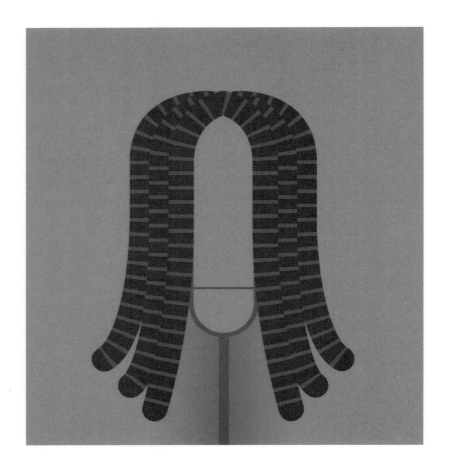

**A**re you white? Do you wish you were black? Do you wear patchwork pants that you made from an old pair of Diesel jeans? If you answered "yes" to these questions, the Trustafarian is right up your street, mon.

Sure, any rich white kid can don an Abercrombie polo with a popped collar, but sometimes you want to embrace other cultures ... or *one* other culture, anyway. So break out your bongos, light up a doobie, and start styling your very own Trustafarian downstairs. After you inhale, lather yourself in a musky, thick layer of patchouli. Light some incense—preferably a woody cypress or juniper— and lock the door. You don't want Mom catching you with the dread wax and your pants down (again). Next, break out your favorite reggae mix tape. Now, grab six to ten miniature rubber bands, dread wax, and a metal comb and start styling: Use the comb to divide your mane into one-inch-by-one-inch sections and secure them with rubber bands. Next, take a dime-size dollop of dread wax and apply to each section. Once each dread has a hearty waxy covering, let your creation rest. Maintain this style with a residue-free shampoo and, of course, ample chillaxing.

# The Mohawk

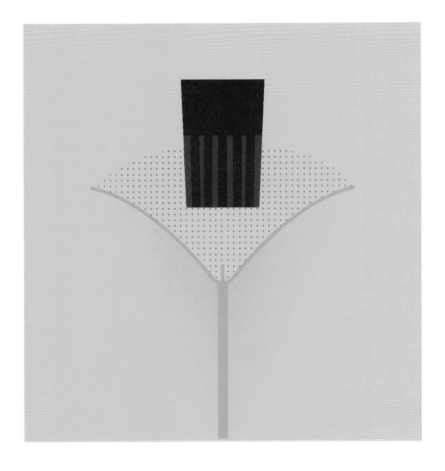

The Mohawk tells the world, "My pubes will not be oppressed by your capitalist authoritarian beliefs."

To style the Mohawk, shave down your pubic hair, leaving a vertical strip of long hair through the middle. The width of this strip is up to you, but an inch is a good starting point. Next, use a flat iron to straighten and lengthen this strip. Then, with both hands covered in styling gel, fashion this middle strip into a Mohawk. You could stop here or you could use scissors to snip the tip of your Mohawk to make it more fanlike.

To properly sport the Mohawk, you need to be unafraid to stand up to oppression. You need to refuse to give in to the fears that our society tries to instill in us. And you need loose pants. After all, you wouldn't want to spend hours perfecting this look, only to squeeze into a tight pair of jeans and ruin all your hard work. But hey, this is your opportunity to start wearing your Hammer pants again, so it's a win-win!

# The Faux Hawk

**D**on't have the stones for a Mohawk? Welcome to the Faux Hawk. To style it, give yourself a short trim all over, leaving about a two-inch-wide vertical strip of long hair through the center of your pubic region. Then take a wad of hair gel and style it into a faux hawk. Now go out there and bend it like faux-hawk fan David Beckham! Then, think about why you have so much trouble with commitment.

# The Peg Bundy

**M**arried ... with Children's Peg Bundy was Al Bundy's sex-crazed, lazy wife, known for her love of bonbons, daytime television, skintight spandex, and, of course, that dazzling fire-engine-red bouffant. With this look downstairs, it won't matter if you're lazy—the lovers will come to you.

If you naturally have a vibrant red patch, congratulations! If not, go to the drug store and buy a box of "Just for Redheads." Once your hair is red, tease up your pubic region with gusto. If you can't get significant volume, invest in a bouffant insert. Once the region has been poofed up and bouffantized, spray approximately one half of an economy-size can of hairspray on it. This will ensure that the red-hot bouffant will stay in place for three to four days—and up to five sexual encounters.

# The American Flag

**A**ttention true patriots: Why wear your flag on your lapel when you can wear it in your pants? To style the American Flag, you'll need a hand or electrical razor; red, white, and blue hair dye; and a deep, deep, *deep* love of your country.

Shave the upper portion of your pubic region into a perfect flag-shaped rectangle. Dye a big blue box in the top left quadrant. Take the red and white dye, and if you're particularly ambitious—or working with a large surface area—dye seven red stripes and six white stripes. If you're working with a smaller canvas, display at least three stripes of each color.

It's star time! I haven't met anyone who had the room to display all 50 stars (and for that I'm grateful) so try the 1777 Continental Congress flag with thirteen stars. And keep in mind that these stars don't have to be perfect; in fact, little white dots will probably suffice.

If this particularly tricky dye job is too rigorous to handle (i.e., you hate freedom and love socialized healthcare), you can always shave "USA" into your botched red, white, and blue canvas.

# The Pepé Le Pube

**A**lthough this style evokes images of the much-loved amorous skunk, Pepé Le Pew, I am certainly not advocating scenting your pubes in a foul-smelling way. Rather, the name refers to the look of the finished style: a center vertical white stripe flanked on each side by a vertical black stripe.

If you have young, jet-black pubes, just dye a vertical white stripe right through the center. If you have old white pubes, do the opposite: Dye your side-pubes black and leave a center strip of white. Blondes, redheads, and those rocking the sophisticated salt-and-pepper pubes will have to dye the whole patch. Add the final touch—speaking in Franglais—and, like the eponymous skunk, your bush will be sweet-talking your lover, as well as any accidentally painted black cats in the area.

# The Elvis

**A**lthough The King died a bloated drug addict, I choose to remember him as a young, vibrant phenomenon with a rockin' hairdo. Though I don't exactly agree with all the style choices he made—sequined unitards among them—I do believe that hair of his was timeless.

To give your crotch a rockin' 'do, take a hefty handful of styling gel and shape your bush into a wave. The style shouldn't be too rigid because, when you shake those hips, you'll want it to bounce a little. And remember, kids, don't make the same mistakes Elvis did: Stay away from drugs and sequined unitards.

# The Bill Clinton

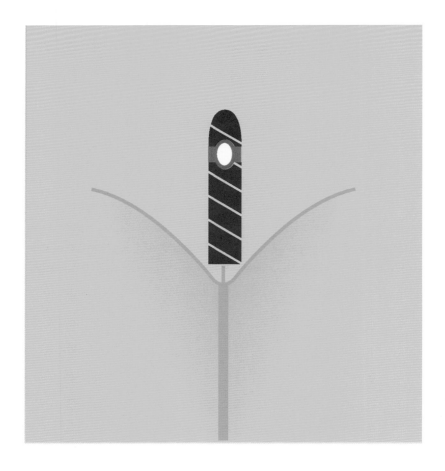

**F**or some, America's 42nd president is remembered not as the Rhodes Scholar who presided over the longest period of peace-time economic expansion in American history, but as the horndog who engaged in some alleged extramarital sex-play with a tubular roll of cured tobacco leaves. And since the former is hard to convey in crotch hair, the Bill Clinton is a patch of pubes shaved in the shape of a cigar.

Since the idea is to make it look like there's a cigar protruding from your privates, this style is best suited for people with vaginas—namely, women. First, give yourself the short trim all over. Next, cut an appropriately sized cigar shape from a piece of heavy paper or poster board. Then place the paper cigar where you'd like your hair-gar to be and shave all the hair around your cutout. Take away the cutout to reveal your tightly cropped, cigar-shaped patch of pubic hair. Then ask your lover to impeach you.

# The Ru Paul

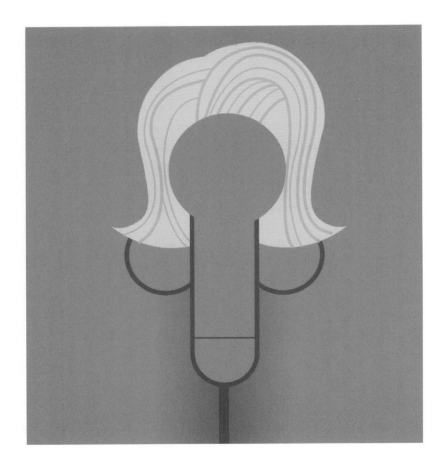

**F**ew are as fabulous as the great Ru Paul. The legs, the heels, the dresses, and—lordy!—that hair. With a tall frame, a tucked member, and an additional foot of platinum blonde hair, Ru Paul is a force to be reckoned with.

If you want your downstairs to scream fabulous blonde tranny, then this style is for you.

First, grow out your entire patch to maximum length. Next, dye your locks a shiny, platinum blonde. What comes next is your own personal Ru Paul expression. Blow-dried straight or moussed up into curls, Ru Paul sports a variety of styles, but one thing is constant—sheer volume and height. Fan out your creation and apply hair spray liberally. In no time at all, your downtown will be dragtastic!

# The Handlebar

**T**he Handlebar is a most dashing cut for any gentleman, meant for those occasions when you're taking a lady to a performance at the local theater or, perhaps, to a moving-picture show. When your damsel pulls down your trousers, she'll know you're a fine suitor upon seeing your "graspable extremities."

To style the Handlebar, first sharpen your straightedge razor* on a piece of leather. Next, take some hot shaving cream and apply it to your private hair. Shave, leaving only a horizontal strip about five to eight inches long, directly above your private parts. Finally, take two dollops of styling gel betwixt the thumbs and forefingers of each hand and style the strip of hair into a handlebar-style mustache. Your crotch will evoke such strong males as William Howard Taft, Archduke Ferdinand, and Josef Stalin and will give your lover something to hold on to.

(*Do not use a straightedge razor.)

# The Imperial

**N**othing says power and authority like the Imperial. Equal parts bravado and manscaping, the Imperial asserts a commanding style. It's similar to the Handlebar, but it's ... more. Much more.

The top of your Imperial should start at the natural top of your patch. From there, shave your locks into a mustache shape—the critical component is the hair horns. The pube-stache must maintain longer locks on the ends, and it should connect to, or at least meet up with, your bushy pubic "sideburns." Gel the ends into two thick, curly wisps. If you want Kaiser Wilhelm in your pants (and who doesn't?), this is the look for you.

# The Alfalfa

**A**lfalfa was the member of "Our Gang" with one of the best-known cowlicks in the business. But if you want to add a little Euro-chic to your crevice, you can tell people this one's called the Tintin.

There are two ways to style the pubic Alfalfa. The first: Using an electric hair trimmer, shave down most of your pubic hair, leaving a patch of long strands. Next, using hair gel, style the patch of long strands into a sprig protruding straight out from the middle of your bush. The second: Instead of shaving down the rest of your pubic hair, simply gel it all down except for a patch of long strands, which you fashion into the sprig. Call this version the Faux-falfa (much like the Faux Hawk is to the Mohawk). Whichever version you choose, your lover will be all over your Little Rascal.

# The Chewbacca

**T**he Chewbacca, simply put, is piles and piles of long, glorious, unadulterated pubes. To pull it off, you have to be blessed with the *Pubis maximus* gene. How do you know if you have this particular gene? Well, does your paternal grandmother have a giant bush? Then you're golden. If not, look into buying a yak hair merkin (see page 110).

This style allows you to explore all kinds of animal noises in the sack with impunity. However, it should be mentioned that, at first, your lover might think that anything nicknamed "Chewie" is less than appetizing in the downstairs area. But once you start walking around with what *Entertainment Weekly* called "one of the greatest sidekicks in film history" between your legs, your partner will definitely owe *you* a life debt.

# The Barrister

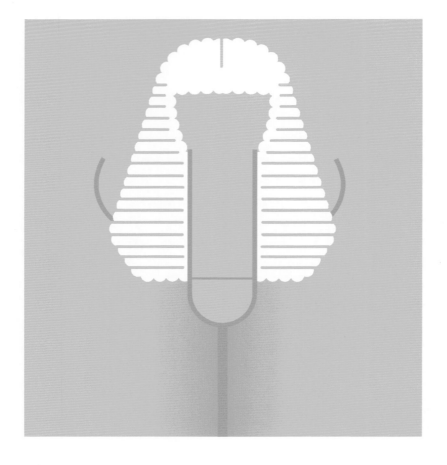

If you want your pleasure zone to be sophisticated, authoritative, and indubitably British, then the Barrister is for you. Fashioned after those adorable little white wigs, this solemn style is intended to indicate to your lover that your crotch is no laughing matter. It's as serious as a heart attack, and sporting a crotch-sized barrister's wig will give you instant confidence and a feeling of superiority.

There are two options for executing the Barrister. First, you can dye your canvas a powder-white color. Next curl up the sides of your nether region and hope it looks legit. For more serious stylists, I recommend crafting an authentic Barrister's wig—merkin style. You can go to your local wig maker, search the local paper, or hit up Craigslist or eBay. Once you obtain an appropriate colonial-style white, you must fashion a piece to fit your personal situation. Once this look is achieved, your crotch is all class, no objections!

# The Flavor Saver

Y ou can think of the Flavor Saver style as the Hitler's smaller, less big-time-Nazi stepbrother. To style your Flavor Saver, simply follow the directions for the Hitler, except crop a tighter square—say one to two centimeters on each side.

The purpose of the Flavor Saver is to save your lover's "flavor," allowing you to catch a whiff of your lover at anytime of the day. Think of it as aromatherapy. Sexy, sexy aromatherapy.

# The Donald Trump

**T**he Donald is known for two things: his money and his hair. You're never gonna have his money, but you *can* have the signature Trump comb-over . . . downstairs.

Okay, here's the art of this deal:

Shave a vertical strip through the center of your pubic bush—roughly two thumb-widths. Add a dollop of styling gel to your remaining pubes. Comb the right half toward the left to cover the now-bare middle strip, being sure to also comb in a slightly downward direction. Continue combing leftward and downward for 15 to 20 minutes until you develop Trump's poofy comb-over look.

Pull this off and you can start referring to your bush as "Mar-a-Lago" and your member as "Trump Tower."

You can take it further by matching your pubic hair color with Trump's goldish-grayish color. This will probably involve color palettes, a paint store, and a professional stylist. I wouldn't go the do-it-yourself route though, folks; it's not easy, and you don't wanna go bankrupt twice doing it. However, if you do succeed, you'll look like a million bucks. We're talking class, here.

# The Marge Simpson

**T**he matriarch of the Simpson family is best known for her grating voice and giant blue beehive hair. Every time I watch that show, I can't help but daydream about what Marge has going on down below. After years of thought, I've decided there's no doubt that her "downstairs hair" is blue. I think it's also obvious that, like her hair, it must protrude—at least a little.

To style the Marge Simpson, you'll need to visit a local drugstore and buy a box of bright blue hair dye. After coloring your pubic hair, your next goal is volume. You want as much horizontal poof as possible. To achieve this, you can tease your hair and hope you're one of the lucky few for whom it works. Alternatively, you can buy a beehive insert.

# The Bull Horns

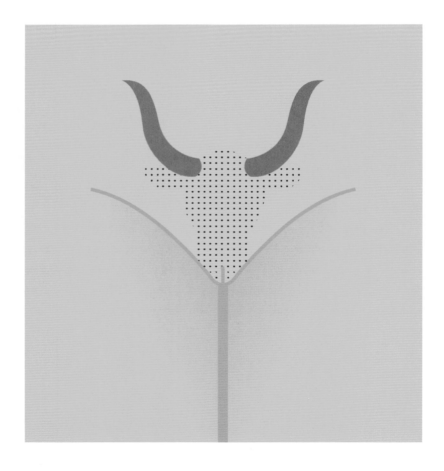

**W**ell howdy, cowboys and girls! I don't know what you consider to be a fun Saturday night, but for me, well there just ain't nothin' better than squeezing into assless chaps and gettin' down and dirty with some farm animals.

I know not everyone has as easy access to farm animals as myself, which is why I suggest the Bull Horns. I can't promise it'll be like riding the real thing, but with some imagination, a nice cowboy get-up, and a rodeo clown in the bed, you'll have a darn-tootin' good time.

To fashion yourself some bull horns, you should first give yourself a short trim. From that point, you can either "free-style" some bull horns with a razor or cut out a stencil in which to fashion the horns. I suggest the stencil; your horns will almost surely be more symmetrical. Once completed, you'll be ready to see how long your partner can hang on to those bull horns and stay on those bucking hips of yours. Yee-haw!

# The Ronald McDonald

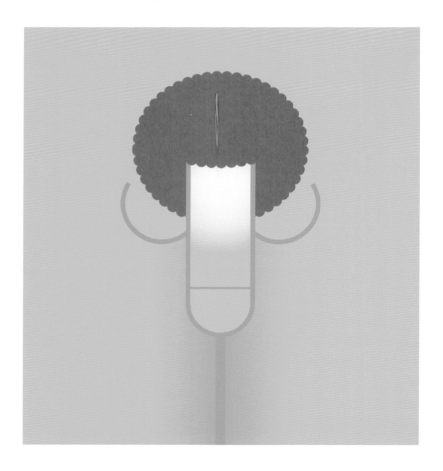

**I** could have selected the Hamburglar, the Grimace, or even those adorable Fry Kids, but it's that strong, kind, masculine Ronny who stole my young heart and left me hungry. Now it's your turn to style the Ronald McDonald on your very own sensual McDonaldland.

To accurately represent Ronny downstairs, you must match color, poof, and energy. Use a vibrant red to dye your entire patch. Next, round the bush with a pair of scissors and use an Afro-comb to really pick out that poof. Finally, if you want to make kids everywhere scream with delight, cover your crotch in chalky white powder and create a smiley face with red clown makeup. I'm lovin' it!

# The Comb-Over

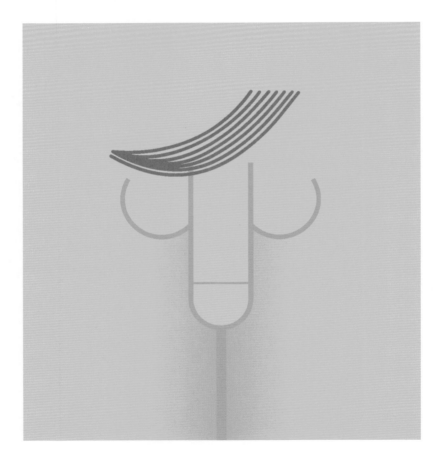

**I**s your bush thinning? Are you experiencing patchy baldness? Face it—it may be time for the comb-over.

If you're already thinning, collect as much of your mop as possible and swoop it to the opposite side. If your locks won't stay put, gel the comb-over so it stays in place. If you have a full mane to work with, grow it out to maximum length, shave half, and repeat the steps for thinning hair.

Sure, comb-overs are associated with creepy old men. But creepy old men are horny, right? Don't you want your privates to conjure up the same kind of naughty filth? The comb-over is like your very own sleazy crotch motel.

# The Rick James

W ith four words—"I'm Rick James, bitch!"—Dave Chappelle reminded us all of the supreme funky majesty of the late super freak. And who wouldn't want the king of funk on their junk?

To have the freakiest down downtown, style the Rick James in one of two ways:

JHERI CURL JAMES: Grow out the sides of your mop. I recommend six inches, if possible. (If not, consider extensions.) Next, take a hearty helping of Jheri curl product and lather your locks to create semicurly, semicrunchy waves. Once you have curly pube-bangs and long curly/crunchy sides, say, "Yow!"

BRAIDED JAMES: Grow your hair in the same fashion. Then create seven to ten miniature braids in your mane (this includes a braided bang region) and secure them with mini rubber bands.

Whichever Rick James you choose, your crotch will never let your spirits dowwwn.

# The Kung Fu Master

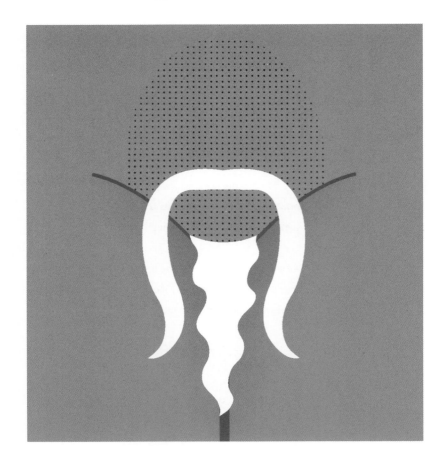

**C**lose your eyes. Be silent. Picture a Chinese kung-fu master's head floating above your crotch. Look carefully at his long, skinny goatee. That is you pubic goal, grasshopper.

To style your Kung Fu Master, shave off all your hair except for a patch. Then take a flat-iron straightener and straighten the patch into a long, flowing goatee. If you have the mental and spiritual power, you can dye the patch white and walk the earth. Either way, with this style, everybody will be kung fu fighting . . . over your crotch!

# The Howard Stern

**H**oward Stern is known for his long curly locks and his obsession with sex. If that sounds like a description you'd like applied to your crotch, pay homage to the king of all media and put Howard on your private parts. (Get it?) It's where he wants to be.

Simply grow out your patch so that it matches Howard's overgrown mane of dark, curly hair. You'll also want to round out the patch with a pair of scissors; Howard's hair always has a rounded look to it. If you want to go Wack Pack crazy, glue a pair of small round sunglasses to your privates. Baba booey!

# The Bride of Frankenstein

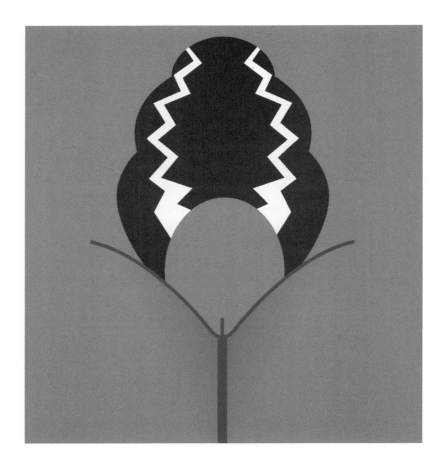

**S**ure zombies and vampires are all the rage, but really, the undead and blood aren't things you really want dancing around your privates. Frankenstein's monster on the other hand, well, now, there's a classy creature with staying power. While there's no denying Frankenstein was a legend in his own right, his bride really stole the show with her iconic tapered lightning-streaked hairdo. If you want to get rough with your lover and let them know you think they're a monster in the sack—bring a little Bride of Frankenstein into the mix.

To style the bride, keep things simple. Grow out your mane to frightening lengths. Use a heavy-duty hairspray to stand the hairs in a tall conical sphere. Next, use white spray hair dye and create two even lightning streaks on each side of your scientific creation.

Once you've sufficiently frightened your follicles, you and your lover will be ready to do the monster mash.

# The Einstein

**P**eople say this Einstein fellow was good at math or philosophy or something, but you know what I say? He was one sexy old coot. Every time I see that white raging mop atop his head, I have visions of the shaggy action he must have had downstairs.

The Einstein is great for the older pube stylist or the younger one who's not afraid to dye his or her patch all white. All you need to do to style the Einstein is grow it out and mess that shit up. In no time your crotch will look brilliant. E equals MC sexy!

# The Kim Jong Il

**A**re you a movie buff, a composer of several operas, and a staunch Stalinist? Then put Kim Jong Il in your pants and show everyone that you have a firm respect for authority.

The first step in styling your very own Kim Jong Il is dying your patch jet black. Then, do a short trim to the outliers of your bikini line to match the tightly cropped band of hair around Kim Jong Il's ears. Finally, you will need to grow out the centermost part of your patch one to two inches and style it up with gel into a meticulously crafted yet effortless-looking bouffant. Glue a pair of large spectacles (or sunglasses, depending on your mood) to your crotch, and your lover will be calling you "Dear Leader" in no time!

# The Shatner

**T**elevision icon, movie star, recording artist, writer, director, spokesperson, serial husband, horse breeder ... William Shatner is a true renaissance man. One way to honor the Shat in your pants is to simply exhibit more hair as you get older, instead of less. But if you don't have a lifetime and your downtown is looking a little bald, grab yourself a very classy and extremely discreet toupee, place it in your private zone, and cut and style it. Keep the Shatner trimmed and combed right to left and apply a dime-size dollop of styling cream. Soon enough, everyone will want to be on the bridge of your Enterprise.

# The Louis Vuitton

**W**hy should rap stars and models get to have all the fun with designer swag from Louis Vuitton? Put the bravado of Kanye between your legs with your own LV logo.

To style your very own designer pubes, you can either use a stencil or do it by hand:

In a straight, clean line, shave downward to start the "L." Complete the bottom portion of the "L" by shaving a shorter, horizontal strip. Start the top of the "V" midway down the "L." Shave the second line of the "V."

Authenticity is key when replicating a Louis Vuitton logo. You don't want anyone to pull down your pants and yell, "Fake!" Believe me, that stays with you.

# The Lightning Bolt

**T**he Lightning Bolt was one of the first innovations in crotch styling, paving the pubic path for all subsequent styles. Therefore, it's important to get this one right. If you do a half-ass job, you'll be disrespecting the entire pubic-hair-styling community. And you do *not* want to get on that shit list.

To style the Lightning Bolt, first use an electric hair trimmer to shave down all your pubic hair to a tight trim. Next, make a stencil by cutting out a lightning-bolt shape from thick paper or poster board. Use the stencil to shave a lightning bolt directly above your privates (or, if you're artistic, do it without the stencil). Maintain that shape with frequent shaving, and your lover will find your crotch electrifying!

# The Cross

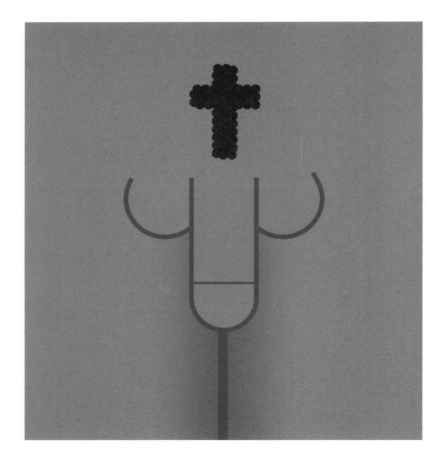

**P**eople often ask me, "What pube style is appropriate for a devout Christian like myself?" The answer, of course, is the Cross. It's the simplest and most accessible of all the Christian pube styles. There's also the Baby Jesus, but I chose not to include it in this book because it's highly complicated and, if attempted by an untrained hand, the results could be . . . apocalyptic.

To style the Cross, first give yourself a short trim. Next, shave a properly proportioned cross directly above your privates. Now just sit back and let your lover get to know you in the biblical sense.

# The Shih Tzu

**S**hih Tzus are special little dogs, and they deserve pubic recognition. To style the Shih Tzu, grow your pubic hair as long as it can go. Then dye some white or tan streaks in there and straighten it all with a straightening iron. Next, spend a good five to ten minutes combing your hair, making sure that it drapes elegantly on each side of your crotch. Glue a little bow in the middle of your bush, and your lover will say, "Holy Shih Tzu, that's adorable!"

# The Crimp

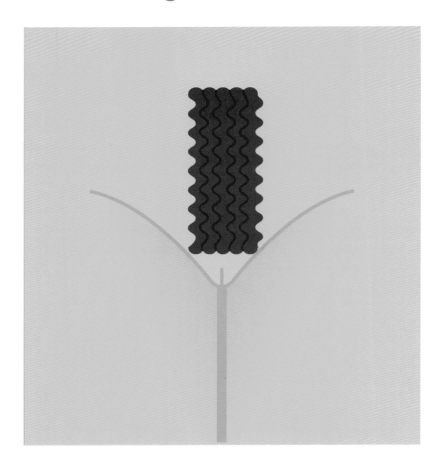

**D**o you want tubular pubulars? Are you brave enough to wield a scalding hot crimping iron downstairs? Then it's crimpin' time! Crimping had its heyday in the '80s and its fabulous unnaturalness will show your lover that you'll go to great lengths to impress.

First, grow those locks to maximum capacity. Mist your entire bush to a slight dampness and then section your patch into three-inch chunks. Begin crimping the hair from the roots and don't stop until the section has maximum drama. Repeat the process for each section and then put on an acid-washed vest (no shirt necessary).

# The Conan O'Brien

**T**he Harvard-educated host of *The Tonight Show* has changed the face of comedy. Why not let him change the face of your privates?

To style the Conan O'Brien, either you need to have been blessed with ginger-tinted pubes or you need to go out and buy some coloring agent. After you have the color down pat, straighten your grown-out bush using a flat iron. Then, brush that hair and simultaneously spray it with hair spray for a solid 30 to 40 minutes. You want some serious lift in that pompadour. Once your mane of ginger hair rises from your crotch like a tsunami, you'll be ready for anything late night.

# The Big Mac

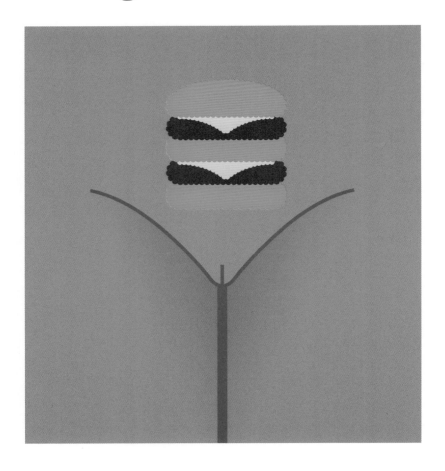

**D**o you have a meat-loving lover and a lot of time on your hands? Then consider an American classic in your crevice: the Big Mac.

McDonald's Big Mac consists of two all-beef patties, special sauce, lettuce, cheese, pickles, onions, and a sesame seed bun. Who wouldn't want to eat that?

To style your own Big Mac, you'll need four dye colors: burger brown (or a natural brunette shade), sesame-seed-bun blonde (or a natural dirty blonde), American-cheese yellow (or pale blonde), and lettuce green. (You can skip the pickles and onions since they're not really visible in the Big Mac profile shot.) Trim your entire pubic patch into a short, even trim. Then dye the eight Big Mac layers as follows:

LAYER 1) Sesame-seed-bun blonde

LAYER 2) Burger brown

LAYER 3) Lettuce green

LAYER 4) Sesame seed-bun blonde

LAYER 5) Burger brown

LAYER 6) Lettuce green

LAYER 7) American-cheese yellow

LAYER 8) Sesame-seed-bun blonde

I recommend using your lover's "Special Sauce" to authenticate the design.

# Frosted Tips

**T**he Frosted Tips pube style is an homage to Food Network's Guy Fieri. To properly style Frosted Tips, you have to nail down the color contrast—a light, crispy blond on the upper level of the hair, and a natural darker color for the rest.

First, shear your crotch to a consistent half-inch length. Once the length is precise, color the top ten percent of each hair. Next, apply a generous amount of low-quality hair gel, like Depp or LA Looks, and gel the shit out of those tips. Your goal is to make your bush as crunchy as the fried zucchini strips this "Food Dude" shills for T.G.I. Friday's.

# Cornrows

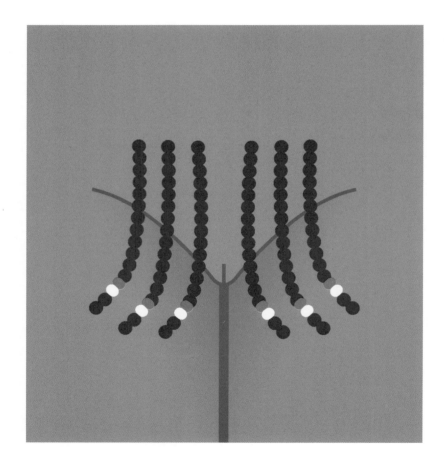

**T**his traditional African style of braiding is not for the novice stylist. It takes dedication and patience to master.

Mist your entire grown-out region until slightly damp, and run a comb through to remove all tangles. Divide your cornrows into four to six sections. Take each section and break it into three even pieces. Braid these pieces, starting from the top down. Make sure you braid tightly and close to the skin. Once you've reached the end of the braid, secure it with a hair accessory, such as a barrette or fabulous snap bead. Repeat these steps for the remaining cornrows, and soon your crotch will look like it just came back from a relaxing Caribbean vacation.

# Extensions

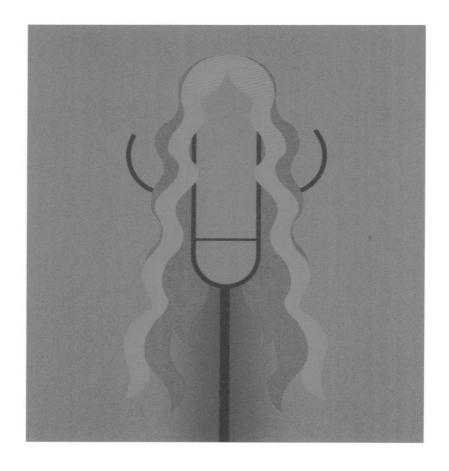

**W**hen you're hitting the club and you want to look fierce, you break out your favorite tube top or leather buttless chaps. But what really gets the party started is a nice natural-looking weave all up in your junk. Paris and Beyoncé always hit up the club with their hair looking luscious, long, and full, so why shouldn't you spoil yourself with a celebrity crotch?

Extensions are a little tricky without professional assistance. You can attempt to integrate them on your own, but for the most authentic look, I recommend visiting a salon with extension experience and that uses 100 percent virgin human hair (donkey or horse hair is a suitable alternative if money is tight). In no time, you'll have a celebrity-style club-hopping crotch you won't be ashamed to flash as you exit your limo!

# Merkins

Though pubic hair is a beautiful thing, the ugly truth is that some of us aren't blessed with it. Whether due to a genetic disease, alopecia, or a tragic crotch fire, some of us can never experience the joy of patch styling. But there are solutions, the least invasive of which are merkins, or pubic wigs. They come in all shapes and sizes, can be custom made, and can even be styled. You can find a merkin dealer on the Internet, but remember, always buy local.

Another option for the pubic-hair impaired is pube plugs. This is a bit more invasive, but you can reap the benefits for many years. Unfortunately, pubic-hair-plug surgery is unavailable in most industrialized nations. But with a little ingenuity, some hiking boots, and a plane ticket to Africa, you'll find someone to re-sod your farm, and you'll once again be able to experience the joys of pubic hair and its maintenance.

# Author Bio

**P**ablo Mitchell leapt from his mother's womb with a comb in one hand and a can of Aquanet in the other. Inspired by high fashion and pop culture, he channeled this energy into his one true passion—the pubic canvas. A rogue member of the underground pubic art scene in the 80s, Pablo broke free from this marginalized group when he began styling the patches of Manhattan's art elite. Soon everyone from Grace Jones to Andy Warhol to Lou Reed were proudly sporting Pablo's signature designs all around town. He opened his first salon in SoHo and then came out with the best-selling line of "Pablo's Soothing Follicular Nourishing Milks." After a brief, regrettable foray into meth, Pablo bounced back to stardom with the reality show Pablo's Pubes. And now comes his greatest treasure of all—*Hip Snips*—so that the common man and woman can have a sweet, sweet taste of glamour, grace, and follicular fabulousness.

**irreference** \ir-'ef-(ə-)rən(t)s\ *n* (2009)

1 : irreverent reference
2 : real information that also entertains or amuses

---

How-Tos. Quizzes. Instructions.
Recipes. Crafts. Jokes.
Trivia. Games. Tricks.
Quotes. Advice. Tips.

Learn something. Or not.

---

**VISIT IRREFERENCE.COM**
The New Quirk Books Web Site